WHAT THE SOLDIE
ON
HADRIAN'S WALL

By

H. RUSSELL ROBINSON, F.S.A.

Coloured paintings by

RONALD EMBLETON, R.O.I.

I.S.B.N. 0 85983 093 4

1976

3rd Edition 1985

Published by
FRANK GRAHAM
6, Queen's Terrace, Newcastle upon Tyne, NE2 2PL

Printed by Howe Brothers (Gateshead) Limited

INTRODUCTION

The Roman army has in recent years received much attention from many eminent European scholars, but much of this has been directed towards its organisation and the history of the frontier systems where most of the army was stationed.

The equipment of the army has only recently been studied in some depth and this mainly in the periods which are best represented by archaeological specimens; the first and early second centuries A.D. This has shed considerable light on the appearance of the legionaries whose new image has been frequently reproduced in recent publications.

I do not therefore intend to describe the arms and armour used by the legions who built Hadrian's Wall in the second century, but to concentrate on recreating the appearance of the provincial auxiliary units who garrisoned the forts, milecastles and turrets of the Wall from the second to fourth centuries.

These soldiers have for too long remained rather shadowy creatures, particularly those who lived in the third and fourth centuries, and the preparation of this booklet has enabled me to at least begin to clarify their outlines and fill in a considerable amount of the detail.

Archaeological excavation along the frontiers of the Roman Empire over the past thirty years has brought to light many remarkable pieces of equipment which have assisted enormously in bringing our auxiliaries to life.

The hadsomely decorated helmets of the cavalrymen, particularly of the late second and early third centuries, the splendid shield bosses and the remarkable succession of finds of their 'sports equipment' have gone a long way towards creating a picture of richness and colour such as we have never imagined existed until quite recently. This splendid equipment was developed no doubt through the growing importance of the cavalryman and the steady decline in the once dominant legionary who stood with both feet planted on the ground and carved out the Roman Empire with his *gladius*.

The auxiliary units were recruited from all over the empire and very often the particular fighting skills of tribesmen or of nationalities were retained and fostered for the benefit of the army and its greater efficiency. Thus we find archers from Syria, slingers from Crete and the Balearic Islands, swift light cavalry from Numidia (Algeria) and heavier cavalry from Spain, Gaul and Thrace (Bulgaria).

Many of these units retained at least an element of their national or tribal armament, though of course such items were eventually Romanised because replacements were made by contractors for the army, not in their country of origin. This can be seen in the helmet of conical Middle Eastern form worn by the Hamian archer on page 33 which is decorated with embossed figures of Roman gods.

The majority of these provincials had to serve for twenty-five years to receive the prized Roman citizenship with an honourable discharge. Their officers gave them their orders in Latin, though Greek was frequently used in the eastern provinces, and their regimental clerks would have written out the rostas and company orders in the same languages. Their names were latinised and their daily routine became that of a typical Roman soldier.

The regiments which garrisoned Hadrian's Wall, with the exception of the Hamians, would not be kept up to strength with recruits brought from the country of origin but with local British tribesmen. These men would come to accept the traditions of their foreign comrades as their own, guarding them as jealously as any of the original men of the regiment would have done.

When one studies the auxiliary forces employed by Rome, one factor very quickly establishes itself and that is that the provincial soldier thought of himself as a Roman and above all else as a Roman soldier, and so too should we. If he died in the service of Rome can we deny him the right to that simple but respected title?

I wish to express my gratitude to Ronald Embleton who has so painstakingly carried out my instructions to provide the splendid series of paintings which have brought this little book to life with a ring of reality and colour. They have indeed brought clarity to the once shadowy forms.

To Dr. David Smith, Keeper of the Museum of Antiquities in the University of Newcastle upon Tyne I wish to record my special thanks, not only for his generous assistance with photographs but also for his inspiring encouragement for any project concerned with the Wall and its environs.

The royalites from this booklet are donated to the Trustees of the Clayton Museum at Chesters fort to be used as they see fit towards the upkeep and improvement of this important collection for it was within the museum surrounded by the fragments of equipment of the Roman garrisons who served there that I first realised the need for this booklet.

ARMS AND ARMOUR OF THE WALL GARRISONS

The Cavalry

Booklet No. 28 in this series describes the Roman Army involved in the building and garrisoning of Hadrian's Wall. The purpose of this booklet is to convey to the reader a more up to date picture of the arms and armour used by these garrisons. This picture can be built up from several sources. Sculpture, Imperial, provincial and military and archaeological finds from Britain and the Continent of Europe, particularly those areas which formed the eastern frontier of the Roman Empire.

The garrisons which occupied the forts, milecastles and turrets of Hadrian's Wall over a period of about two hundred and eighty years, were changed from time to time though some may have remained in one station throughout almost the whole period of occupation. One of the last could have been the thousand strong *ala Augusta Gallorum Petriana milliaria civium Romanorum*, the largest cavalry unit in Britain and known to have been stationed on the northern frontier at Corbridge (*Corstopitum*) before A.D.98 from whence the monks of Hexham later removed a military gravestone with other masonry when building their Abbey. The gravestone, like the few others surviving from the Wall area, has been badly worn and consequently lost much of its detail. It is in the traditional style of cavalry gravestones of the first century showing the horseman in a pillared *aedicula* with a fallen barbarian below the galloping horse. From the inscription beneath we learn that this cavalryman was Flavinus, standard bearer of the troop of Candidus (decurion, troop commander) of the *ala Petriana*.

A close and careful study of the worn relief reveals something to the observer. Flavinus wears a helmet with a high curved crest with large standing feathers at the side. These crests suggest that the helmet could be one of the masked variety as worn for cavalry displays for they are seldom seen on field headpieces. As we know from other contemporary grave *stelae*, armoured cavalry wear mail (*lorica hamata*) or scale armour (*lorica squamata*) for the defence of the body. As scales are nowhere suggested we may assume that his body armour was of mail, the untextured surface simply being painted grey to depict iron mail with bands of another colour on the upper arms and around the edge of the skirt where his under tunic showed. His legs would have been painted to represent tight breeches reaching to below the knee.

Gravestone of Flavinus, standard bearer of the troop of Candidus of the *ala* Petriana who died when twenty-five years of age after serving for seven years. Hexham Abbey.

Photograph by J. E. Hedley, Corbridge

econstruction of
e equipment of
lavinus

Ronald Embleton

We can also make out the forward edge of an oval shield (*clipeus*) behind the horse's head and the cavalryman's long sword (*spatha*) suspended at his right side, probably on a waist belt. In his right hand, Flavinus carries the standard of his *turma* which appears to be a staff surmounted by a disc containing a head surrounded by radiating points, a standard resembling the *imago* carried by Roman units bearing a likeness of the reigning emperor. As Flavinus is called a *signifer* and not an *imaginifer* we may assume that the head on his standard is that of some deity particularly sacred to the men of the *ala Petriana*.

The equipment described above is typical of the Roman auxiliary cavalry throughout most of the northern frontier history. The ordinary cavalryman would have carried a lance (*hasta*) and/or a number of lighter javelins for throwing which the Jewish historian, Flavius Josephus, in the time of Vespasian (A.D.69-79), describes as being carried in a quiver attached to the saddle.

Cavalry regiments were stationed on the Wall at Halton, Chesters and Stanwix and from the early 3rd century at Benwell and for a time in the second century, at South Shields. These were the elite regiments of the northern frontier and the best equipped. By the fourth century cavalry had become more important than the legions which were reduced in size to about 1,000 men and largely relegated to the status of frontier guards; a role originally filled by the non-citizen auxilia.

Cavalry equipment remained basically unchanged and it was generally only the form of the helmet by which one could distinguish the period to which a trooper belonged. By the third century long sleeved tunics and by the fourth century long trousers tucked into the boots, somewhat changed the appearance of the Roman soldier; changes no doubt brought about by the German tribesmen who filled the ranks of western armies in ever increasing numbers, and to some extent, the influence of the east where such fashions had long existed.

Changes in equipment were probably very slow but patterns would appear to have varied from one part of the Roman Empire to another. Another factor to be taken into consideration would be the different materials and techniques used by the various contractors who supplied the frontier troops before the establishment of Imperial arms factories (*fabricae*) under Diocletian in the late third century.

The earliest cavalry helmet to survive from Britain's northern frontier comes from Newstead (*Trimontium*) near Melrose and dates from the end of the first period of the fort which was probably over-run or evacuated between A.D. 98 and 100 (page 7). It is a simple iron skull-piece extended well down at the back of the neck with a narrow projecting flange at the lower edge. It was originally sheathed in tinned bronze embossed on top of the skull to represent hair; a type of cavalry helmet shown in numerous grave reliefs from the Rhine frontier. A more complete specimen was found at Koblenz-Bubenheim in 1961 (page 7).

Fragments of an iron cheek-piece with an outer covering of embossed bronze, from a helmet of the same type were also found at Newstead and other more complete specimens of the outer bronze plates are at Corbridge and Carlisle (page 9).

The equipment of the early second century is only covered by the sculpture commemorating the triumphs of Trajan's army over the Dacians and this has to be used with discretion. Although the Trajan Column at Rome shows auxiliary troops, both horse and foot, armed in the same manner without distinction, archaeological evidence points to differences between cavalry and infantry equipment throughout the first and later second centuries. To the artists who created the cartoons from which the sculptors carved the reliefs, the differences between types of helmet, etc., may not have been so apparent (page 11). It is the author's opinion that cavalry helmets would have certainly maintained the greater depth at the back already apparent in the first century and on

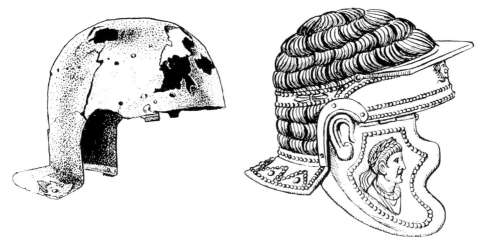

Cavalry helmets of the late 1st century A.D.
  (*Left*) Iron skull of a helmet from the fort at Newstead. Museum of Antiquities, Edinburgh
  (*Right*) Reconstruction of a helmet found at Koblenz-Bubenheim. Koblenz City Museum

later second century specimens where they are extended even nearer the base of the neck with a greater flange to guard the shoulders.

Early in the second century many helmets, both legionary and auxiliary, have their crowns reinforced with crossed strips of iron or bronze. A portion of one of these bronze reinforcing strips which can be dated to the time of Antoninus Pius (A.D. 138-161) was found in the fort at Newstead. Similar reinforces, all of bronze, have been found at Corbridge and Chesters some retaining their tall conical rivets by which they were attached (page 11). Portion of a bronze peak from a cavalry helmet has also been found at Corbridge (see same illustration). A complete helmet of iron with bronze fittings from the fort at Heddernheim and now in the Frankfurt Museum is shown on page 13.

A splendid cheek-piece from a bronze helmet found at South Shields (page 14) now in the Museum of Antiquities of Newcastle, is decorated with a Dioscurus (one of the twins, Castor and Pollux), a dolphin and some leaf and floral motifs applied with a punch. It has been subjected to alteration by trimming off some of the rear edge and the protective out-turned throat flange of the lower edge. A bronze cavalry helmet from Bodegraven in Holland and now in the Rijksmuseum van Oudheden, Leiden (page 14) which can be dated to the late second or early third centuries, bears similar leaf ornament in its engraved decoration and there can be little doubt that it is from a helmet of this pattern that the cheek-piece originally came. A more complete specimen of the same date and fashion but made of iron with applied bronze ornamental fittings also from the fort at Heddernheim near Frankfurt, is shown on page 15. It is only when we see the richness and high standard of these troopers' helmets that he begin to realise how splendidly they could be equipped.

All helmets, for both cavalry and infantry, were fitted with carrying handles. These were like the Victorian loop drawer-handle attached by two split-pins at the centre of the neck-guard. Examples of helmet-handles of the late second and third centuries are exhibited at Corbridge in the site museum and a late specimen can be seen at South Shields (page 15).

By the fourth century, eastern influences have changed many features of Roman equipment so much that they are barely recognisable. Rome had always been prepared to copy the equipment of her enemies if it proved superior to her own and it may simply be that when the new field armies were being developed to oppose the ever increasing

7

Decurion and troopers of a cavalry *ala*, 3rd century A.D.

raids in the east from Goths and Huns, the large cavalry element was armed in a similar manner to Rome's more eastern neighbours who specialised in mounted warfare.

The fourth century helmet had a hemispherical bowl made in two halves joined with a raised comb or ridge from front to back. At the front a nasal or nose-guard was attached with metal eye-grows on either side. The cheeks and sides of the head were guarded by long cheek-pieces and a small rounded neck-guard was hung by straps at the back. Examples are known cased in gold and set with semi-precious stones or with sheets of embossed silver whilst others are sheathed in gilt bronze. Only a fragment of one of these helmets has been found in Britain; an iron neck-guard bordered with bronze strip which was found in the Saxon Shore fort at Richborough (*Rutupiae*) in Kent and is now to be seen in the site museum (page 16). These helmets show strong Persian influence in their form and construction and in their turn influenced Scandinavian helmets of the seventh century such as that found in the Sutton Hoo ship burial now in the British Museum. A silver sheathed example at Leiden is shown on page 16.

Cavalry body armour normally consisted of a short sleeved mail shirt reaching to the hips. The borbers were either straight or dagged in a series of points. Some units had scale shirts of either iron or bronze. Scales, which were made in a great variety of sizes, were linked together into horizontal rows with loops of bronze wire and then sewn onto a linen garment, each row overlapping the row beneath by about one third. Some

8

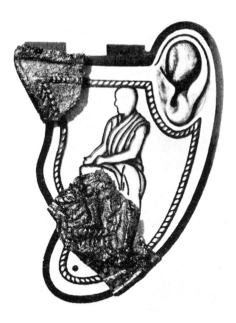

Newstead, late 1st century

Carlisle, 3rd century

Corbridge, 2nd century

Photograph University Library and Museum of
Antiquities, Newcastle upon Tyne

scales such as a group found at Corbridge which are 1·5 cm. long by 1·00 cm. wide, are very small (page 18) whilst others, of more common size, are 2·5 cm. long by 1·5 cm. wide (page 18). There were also scales of very much greater size such as those used for the mid third century horse armours found at Dura Europos. These have scales averaging 3·5 cm. long by 2·5 cm. wide. It has been suggested by some authorities that scale shirts were made up of scales of different sizes to make the fitting of sleeves and neck openings more practicable but most large pieces found so far do not bear this theory out.

Scale armour was never as strong and durable as mail therefore *lorica squamata* could not be made too long in the skirt particularly for horsemen. Some were finished at the level of the wearer's hips while others terminated at the waist below which the body was protected by a skirt of stout pendant leather straps (*pteruges*). The short sleeves might also be replaced with a series of shorter straps attached around the armholes of the scale body armour.

In the third century another form of body armour was introduced from the Middle East where it had been used for many centuries. This was lamellar armour built up of long narrow scales with rounded heads joined both horizontally and vertically with leather laces. The rows of lamellae overlapped upwards, the opposite to scales, making the garment very much more flexible. As the lamellae were often made of lacquered rawhide it was also very much lighter. Two thigh defences made of rawhide lamellae were found at Dura Europos. They were practically complete and had once formed part of a mid third century *clibanarii* equipment. *Clibanarii* were completely armoured riders on armoured horses sometimes referred to as *cataphractarii*. They were used in large numbers by the Persians and Parthians and to some extent by the Romans. Although of a very unusual type, lamellae have been found at Corbridge (page 18). They are of extremely small size, one group being 2·5 cm. long by 0·7 cm. wide and an even smaller group being 1·8 cm. long by 0·5 cm. wide. These little plates must have once formed part of a fourth century officer's *lorica* of a type depicted in traditional ikons showing military saints of the Greek Orthodox Church which remained in fashion for a long time in Byzantium.

The Roman cavalry sword was the *spatha*, the long Celtic cutting sword of La Tene III type. When Rome began to enlist Gauls and Celtiberians as auxiliary cavalry in the first century B.C. they continued to use their native equipment and it was not until the establishment of the principate of Augustus that the auxilia was properly established as part of the Roman army. Throughout the first century A.D. auxiliary cavalry are represented in sculpture as wearing a standard Romanised equipment including Gallic mail shirt, oval or hexagonal Celtic shield and the long Celtic sword. The only difference is that they are equipped from workshops under the direction of Roman officials which gives every element a Roman character.

Two fine *spathae* blades have been found in the rubbish pits in the fort at Newstead and are now in the Musuem of Antiquities at Edinburgh (page 19). As no hilts have survived with them the illustration shows one restored with a hilt of bone which was found at Nijmegen in Holland and now in the Rijksmuseum G.M.Kam. Cavalry swords average about 62·5 cm. long with a width of 3·5 cm.

The lance *hasta* was used by both horse and foot. It could be wielded in the hand or thrown, but one assumes that it was retained in action as long as possible. Its overall length was probably between 1·82 m. and 2·73 m. whilst the long Partho-Persian *contus* used by some Roman cavalry was bout 3·64 m. The long lances were of course intended as shock weapons but without stirrups horsemen were restricted in the amount of force and weight that they could put behind a couched lance. Almost all sculptured representations of Roman cavalrymen show them as if either throwing their spears or stabbing downwards with an overarm action and only one example of a couched lance is known to the author. This is in a combat scene on the Arch or Orange.

Auxiliary cavalry and infantry from Trajan's Column, Rome, early 2nd century A.D. All wear simple helmets, mail shirts and carry oval shields.

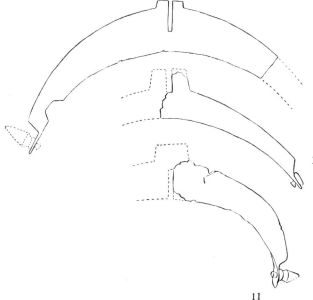

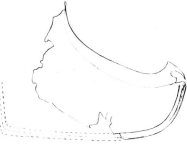

Fragments from cavalry helmets.

A. & B. Reinforces from Corbridge, mid 2nd-early 3rd centuries. Corbridge site museum

C. Reinforce from Newstead, mid 2nd century. Museum of Antiquities, Edinburgh

D. Left half of a bronze peak from Corbridge. Corbridge site museum

A fine series of late first century lance heads comes from Newstead and shows a very much higher standard of finish to the third and fourth century group found in Chesters fort and now exhibited there in the Clayton Museum (page 22). Similar late spear heads have been found in the fort at Richborough in Kent. Lance heads are generally leaf-shaped and range from 25-35 cm. in length. Javelins would have an overall length of from 91-150 cm. varying in weight according to the size of the head (page 19). Lances, spears and javelins all had iron shoes at the butt-end of their shafts, generally pointed, to act as a counter balance to the head, for sticking in the ground and as an additional offensive point (page 22). Fragments of shafts found in the sockets of heads from Newstead showed that they had been made of hazel wood.

The cavalry shield of the first and second centuries was flat and either oval or an elongated hexagon. It was of laminated construction, rather like modern ply-wood covered at front and back with thin sheep or goat skin and bound at the edge with metal, usually bronze. It would appear that each unit had its own device or pattern which was painted on the front of the shields but whether the colour of the background was the same for the whole regiment or varied from *turma* to *turma*, we do not know. The hemispherical boss (*umbo*) was attached by four or six rivets at the centre of the shield where the single horizontal hand-grip was situated. These bosses could be of plain bronze simply decorated with engraved concentric rings like one found at Matfen, just east of Haltonchesters (page 22), but now unfortunately lost. Others were richly engraved and frequently tinned to give a bright silver background to the yellow bronze ornament. A fine engraved boss was found at Kirkham in Lancashire and is now in the British Museum and other splendid specimens retaining much of their original colour have been found on the Continent (page 23).

Five oval shields were found at Dura Europos on the Euphrates dating from the mid third century, three of which were so elaborately painted they must have been made for use in cavalry displays. They are broader ovals than earlier examples, 1·07-1·18 m. long by 0·92-0·97 m. wide. They are slightly convex and built up of narrow poplar boards glued edge to edge and bound at the outer rim with leather (page 23).

Tinning or silvering and sometimes gilding, was lavished on the decorated armour made specially for the *Hippika Gymnasia* or cavalry displays. These events were given, as far as one can judge, on religious holidays, the emperors birthday and for such occasions as the visits of a provincial governor. They were no doubt also used to impress the "natives" when it was felt that someone needed reminding of the superiority of Roman military strength, Flavius Arrianus, known to scholars as Arrian, who was governor of Cappadocia under Hadrian, has left a most remarkable account of the *hippika gymnasia* in his *Tactica*. He describes everything from the preparation of the ground right through to the end of the display. It commenced with a dashing entry with streaming plumes and standards after which came several demonstrations of javelin throwing with half the troop attacking the other half, all the attacks being delivered at full gallop. After these spectacular performances came daring exhibitions of target practice with the riders throwing their javelins from the moment they commenced their run-in and spinning their mounts to deliver their last missile backwards into the target. Also described is the Cantabrian circle in which a troop of horsemen rode in a ring past two stationary riders who guarded themselves with their shields against a constant shower of javelins.

The colour, the clatter of javelins on shields, the dust from the pounding hoofs and the cheering of the enthralled and excited spectators are now lost to us but the broken and tarnished remains of their gay sports equipment can still stir the imaginations of those who have had the opportunity to study this interesting aspect of the Roman army. The helmets with their richly embossed skulls and their severe classical masks, the embossed breastplates and greaves for the riders' shins and the chamfrons and breast ornaments for the horses have all survived in considerable quantity. One large hoard found at Straubing on the Danube and dating from the first half of the third century provides us with a remarkable picture of this equipment used at that time. Helmets were made to represent either male or female and it is possible that the two divisions represent-ed Greeks and Amazons, a favourite subject of Greek legend passed down to the Romans with Hellenistic traditions and used to decorate one of the painted Dura shields.

The northern frontier has already delivered up some splendid treasures once used in these displays of skill. The finest came from Newstead and consisted of two late first century helmets; one of bright yellow brass and the other of iron, which though damaged, retained its mask. There was also a female mask of bronze from another helmet (page 26). A piece of laminated bronze armour found in a very fragmentary state has proved, after careful restoration, to be a thigh defence for a horseman rather similar in outline to the lamellar pieces found at Dura Europos. It is however too light for field use but would turn a headless sports javelin (page 28).

A unique find at Newstead was a thick leather chamfron or horse helmet, decorated with tooling and bronze studs of various sizes and portions of a second example (page 28). Both lacked protection for the horses' eyes but vacant rivet holes around the circular eye-openings show where the metal eye-guards were attached. None were found at Newstead but two sites in the Wall area have examples which help us to complete the picture. One is in the Corbridge site museum and is farily complete (page 28). It consists of a low circular dome pierced with a trellis pattern with a surrounding flange pierced for riveting to the leather chamfron (page 30). The second is only a fragment of a similar piece from the fort at Chesters and can now be seen in the museum there.

No other sports equipment has yet been found on the Wall sites but it is still possible that opportunities to dig in the area of *Petriana* (Stanwix) may bring to light rich elements of this exciting and unusual equipment such as have been found at Newstead in Scotland and in more southern stations of the Empire. A reconstruction of cavalrymen of the third century armed for the *hippika gymnasia* is shown on page 17.

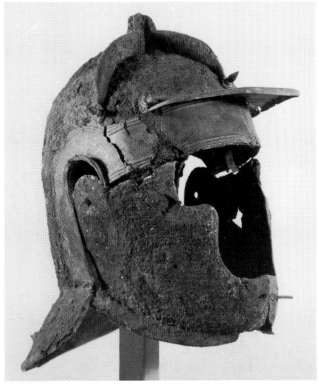

Iron cavalry helmet with bronze mounts from Heddern-heim, 2nd half 2nd century. Frankfurt Museum

Bronze cheek-piece from a cavalry helmet decorated with a figure of a Dioscurus, late 2nd- early 3rd centuries. From the fort at South Shields. Museum of Antiquities, Newcastle upon Tyne.

Photograph, University Library and Museum of Antiquities, Newcastle upon Tyne

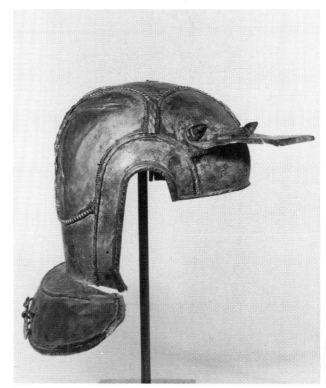

Bronze cavalry helmet, late 2nd-early 3rd centuries. It bears similar engraved decoration to the South Shields cheek-piece.

Rijksmuseum van Oudheden te Leiden

Iron cavalry helmet with bronze decoration and fittings, late 2nd-early 3rd centuries. It lacks its peak and left cheek-piece. From Heddernheim.

Franfurt Museum

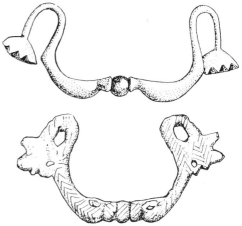

Carrying handles for helmets.

A. & B.   From Corbridge, site museum

C.   From South Shields, site museum

Iron neck-guard from a 4th century helmet, from the Saxon Shore fort at Richborough, Kent. Site museum

Silver sheathed iron cavalry helmet, 4th century, from Deurne, North Brabant.

Rijksmuseum van Oudheden te Leiden

(*Opposite*) Cavalry equipped for the *hippika gymnasia*, 3rd century A.D.

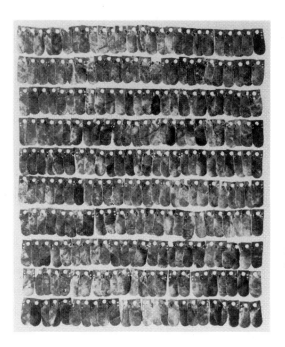

Bronze armour scales from Newstead. Museum of Antiquities, Edinburgh.

Small bronze armour scales from Corbridge, site museum.

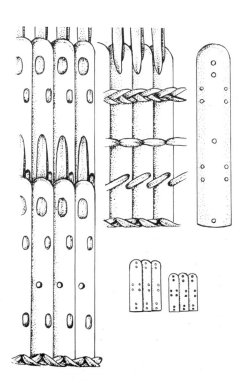

Lamellar armour.

(*Left*)   Section of Tibetan iron lamellar armour laced with buckskin, outside.

(*Centre*)   The same, inside.

(*Right*)   Single lamella

(*Bottom*)   Small Lamellae from Corbridge, 3rd-4th centuries. Site museum.

Roman swords.

(*Top*)   Auxiliary cavalry *spatha* reconstructed with a blade from Newstead and a bone hilt from Nijmegen in Holland.

(*Bottom*) The infantry *gladius*.

Both late 1st or early 2nd centuries

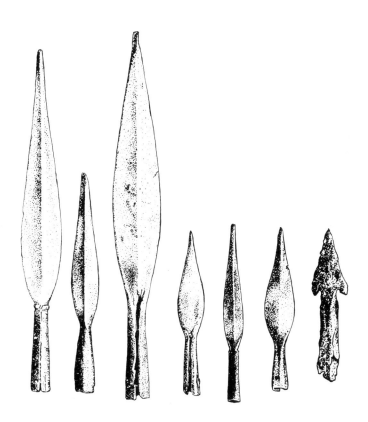

Lance and javelin heads from Newstead, late 1st-early 2nd centuries. Museum of Antiquities, Edinburgh

(*Above*) Centurion and soldiers of an infantry cohort, 2nd century.

(*Right*) Irregular scouts and Raetian auxiliaries, 3rd century.

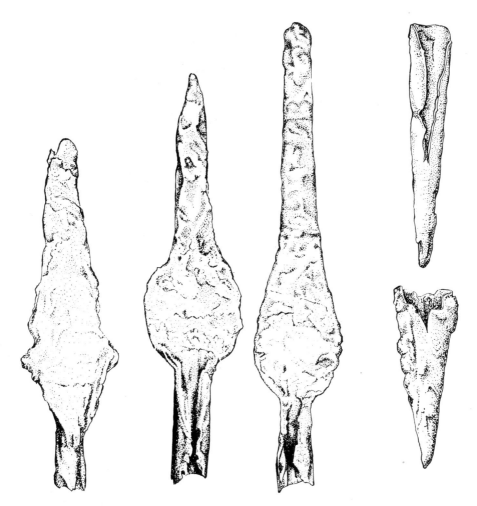

Spear heads from the fort at Chesters, 3rd-4th centuries. Site Museum. Spear butts from Carrawburgh and Corbridge.

Bronze shield boss found at Matfen in the 19th century. Present whereabouts unknown.

Shield boss with engraved decoration from Kirkham, Lancs. British Museum.

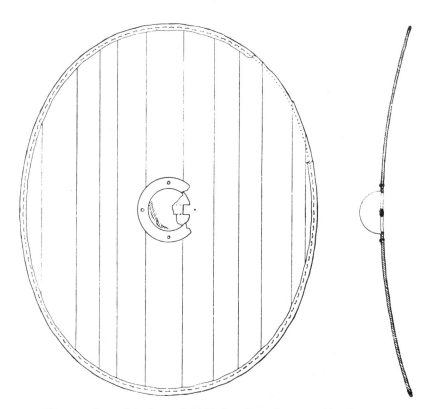

Diagram of one of the five oval shields from Dura Europos, mid 3rd century.

23

The Infantry Cohorts

The auxiliary infantry cohorts normally consisted of either ten (*milliaria*) or five (*quingenaria*) centuries each of 80 men under a centurion and an *optio*, the centurion's aide.

The equipment varied little from the service arms and armour we have discussed for the cavalry except that their helmets were of a more simple kind and considerably less deep at the back and their swords were the short *gladius*. The helmets that survive which may possibly be allocated to the auxiliary *pedites* are simplified versions of those worn by the legionaries. None of these have survived in Britain so that we must look at Continental finds to obtain some idea of their form. The best example, made of bronze, was found in the Rhine at Mainz and is probably of the late first or early second centuries. It is approximately of the same form as contemporary legionary helmets but without any of the applied or embossed ornament. Only the essentials are attached; a reinforcing peak set high on the brow, projecting ear-guards and plain hinged cheek-pieces (page 30). It is probably of a type which remained long in use but we have only one example of succeeding types and this we shall discuss under *cohors equitata*.

Body armour was generally the short mail *lorica hamata* such as we see on the columns of Trajan and Marcus Aurelius at Rome. On the Marcus Column many of the infantry are shown in scale *lorica squamata* of the same 'cut' as the mail shirts. Such differences in equipment were probably due to the area in which a unit was stationed and the type of armour, etc., which the local craftsmen specialised in making.

Shields, like those of the cavalry, are generally oval with similar hemispherical bosses covering the recess for the central grip. Teutonic units are known to have used tall conical bosses with or without button finials similar to those brought to Britain in later times by Saxon invaders (page 30). All shields were fitted with goatskin covers and we are able to ascertain the exact size of shields from these. Mid first century oval covers from the fort at Valkenburg in Holland show a size of 128 cm. by 66 cm. (page 34).

The infantry sword was the same as the legionary *gladius*, a weapon with a blade 49·5 cm. long by 5·00 cm. wide, furnished with a richly decorated scabbard in the first century but by the second, carried in a simple sheath of leather covered wood protected with a metal frame to which the suspension rings were attached. The sword belt was a narrow baldric worn over the left shoulder with the sword worn fairly high on the right side. This *balteus* was divided at the back and secured to the two rings on the rear edge of the sheath and at the front only the upper of the two rings was employed.

The remains of an infantry *gladius* blade was found in the fort at South Shields and this is now exhibited in the site museum there, sealed in a plastic case to keep it in a stable condition since its skilful cleaning in the British Museum laboratory. All that survives is about the upper third of the blade, and below the shoulders where once the hilt was fitted there are interesting inlays in yellow bronze. On the obverse face there is a figure of Mars, the God or War and on the reverse, a legionary eagle flanked by cohort standards (page 34). Similar inlays can be seen on both short and long Roman swords found in Scandinavia and Poland; swords which have found their way beyond the Roman controlled frontier through trade or capture on the Rhine. These weapons date from the late second and early third centuries.

There is no sculptural evidence for legionaries or auxiliary infantry carrying daggers (*pugio*) in the second century but a large quantity of these weapons were found in the third century fort of Kastell Künzing in Germany. The daggers are mostly of large size being some 40·00 cm. long and of the same pattern as one found in Copthall Court in the City of London and now in the Museum of London (page 35). Such daggers may have replaced the sword with some units though it should be noted that some very short swords were also included in the Künzing hoard.

PLATE XXIX

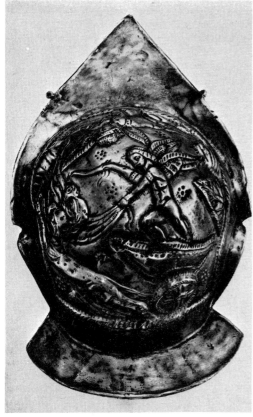

Helmets for cavalry displays from Newstead.

Above)   Helmet of brass lacking its mask

(*Right*)   Helmet of iron with mask

(*Bottom*)   Mask of bronze

All late 1st century

Museum of Antiquities, Edinburgh

A dedication stone from Birdoswald fort which housed the *cohors I Aelia Dacorum* in the third and fourth centuries, bears a relief of a typical curved Dacian sword which could have been carried by this unit as its traditional native weapon. The form of the blade shown suggests some modification for it no longer displays the sickle-like quality of the Dacian weapons on the Trajan Column. It has also been given more of a true sword hilt instead of the straight handle of the old native weapon (page 35).

Infantry spears were similar in every respect to those used by the cavalry. First century grave reliefs show soldiers carrying two spears which were the alternative to the two *pila* of the legionaries. They were probably thrown at the opening of an engagement but one might have been retained and wielded in the hand as long as conditions permitted. Some units may have used javelins of smaller size which could have been carried in larger quantities.

A rather crude relief of an infantry soldier found at Carrawburgh is now to be seen in the Clayton Museum at Chesters (page 33). It is possibly part of a gravestone though it lacks the usual architectural features one would expect to find on such a stone. It is of particular interest for it represents a *signifer* or standard bearer wearing a bear skin over his helmet and shoulders and bearing the standard in his right hand the head of which is a bull, possibly the totem of his unit, with a trident-like shoe at the butt for planting it in the ground. His unusual shield may represent a small version of the type carried by the tribes from which his cohort was originally recruited. At his left side hangs his *gladius* and around the waist of his very full tunic is a belt with a long hanging end. The presence of a *gladius* tells us that the relief cannot be later than the first half of the third century for after that time the *spatha* replaces the shorter weapon.

The Cohors Equitata (mixed cohorts)

These units of five-hundred or a thousand strong were part infantry and part cavalry, the cavalry being the senior section of the cohort and therefore the better paid. However this cavalry element was not as well paid as the troopers of the cavalry *alae*. This is made very clear in Hadrian's *adlocutio* or address to his troops at Lambaesis in the Province of Numidia (Algeria) after each unit had demonstrated their skills in various field exercises.

To the Sixth Cohort of Commagene (north-west Syria) he said:— "It is difficult for the cavalry of a part mounted cohort to give satisfaction in any case, more difficult for them not to cause dissatisfaction after the manoeuvre of a cavalry regiment. The area of the parade ground is different and so is the number of javelin throwers; the quality of your horses and your arms correspond with your lower pay. But you have avoided contempt by your keenness in doing what had to be done with vigour. To this you have added throwing stones with slings and combat with missiles. You have on all occasions jumped with alacrity. The special care of my distinguished legate Catullinus is apparent in your quality under his command".

Two bronze helmets have survived dating from the late first or early second centuries. Both are of the same deep form with slightly pointed skulls, embossed ear-guards and small projecting neck-guards. They have both lost their cheek-pieces and applied peaks but display an overall simplification which indicates an inferiority to helmets worn by men of the cavalry *alae*. One of these helmets in the Archaeological Museum at Zagreb is shown on page 37.

A helmet, probably worn by the infantrymen of mixed cohorts in the second century is now in the Archaeological Museum at Florence. It has been subjected to alteration and now survives as a low hemispherical bowl with crossed reinforces, a flat peak at the front and flanged cut-outs over the ears. The neck-guard has been cut away and the cheek-pieces removed, but originally it was probably like the reinforced auxiliary helmets depicted in the reliefs on Trajan's Column. The original is illustrated on page 38 with a probable reconstruction.

Reconstruction of a laminated bronze thigh-guard from Newstead by the author. Late 1st century.

Museum of Antiquities, Edinburgh

Pierced bronze eye-guard for a chamfron from Corbridge. Site Museum.

Photograph, University Library and Museum of Antiquities, Newcastle upon Tyne

Chamfron for a horse of thick leather. From Newstead.   Museum of Antiquities, Edinburgh

From the later second century or early third, two cavalry helmets have been found which exhibit all the characteristics of the contemporary cavalry *alae* head-pieces as shown on page 13 but they are made of bronze with the ear-guards formed on one with the skull-piece. The reinforces are inferior in finish as is the thin peak applied at the front. The best of these is in a private collection in Germany and came from Hönnepel near Kleve. A pair of large cheek-pieces from a helmet of this type was found at Konigshofen near Strasbourg (page 37).

Cohors Sagittariorum

A corps of archers, the *I Hamiorum sagittariorum* was stationed at Carvoran at the end of the reign of Hadrian and in the 160's under Marcus Aurelius. They were at Bar Hill during the second occupation of the Antonine Wall in Scotland.

A gravestone to one of these Syrians was found at Housesteads which can be dated to between A.D. 125 and 140 but it is not known whether any of this unit were ever detached for duty there. This grave relief, now in the Museum of Antiquities at Newcastle, is very worn but shows the soldier in a conical helmet and probably wearing a mail shirt. On his back is slung a quiver of arrows and on his waist-belt, at the right side, hangs a large knife. His bow, of recurved composite type, is in his left hand and a small axe is in his right (page 32). Eastern cavalry are described by Arrian as being armed with bows and small axes with round cutting edges. It is interesting to note that Scythian archers in the service of the ancient Greek states are frequently represented carrying similar axes as a secondary weapon.

A remarkable conical bronze helmet of the type used by Levantine auxiliaries, was found at Bryastovets in Bulgaria and is now in the Archaeological Museum, Sofia. It is embossed with the deities Mercury, Apollo, Minerva, Victory and Mars, each standing within an arched *aedicula*. The remaining cheek-piece carries the figure of Neptune. The raised decoration was in yellow bronze standing out in contrast against the tinned background. There was originally a curtain-like neck-guard of scale-covered fabric attached at the back as indicated by the series of holes in the rear edge of the skull-piece. Another conical helmet of bronze with its brow-plate embossed with figures of Victory, Jupiter and Mars, is now in the Archaeological Museum, Zagreb. The pattern of the narrow applied borders indicates that it dates from the late second or early third centuries (page 37).

The horn reinforces for the long curved "ears" of composite reflex bows, have been found on a number of sites in Britain including the Antonine fort at Bar Hill where the Hamians were stationed for a time, in the military depot at Corbridge and in some quantity in the third century workshops at Caerleon in South Wales. The bows were built up of wood and sinew glued together and these bone plates were stuck on either side of the wooden "ears" to strengthen them and also reinforce the nocks for the bow-string cut in their forward edge (page 39). The bow-string was drawn back by the archer with a bone or bronze ring worn on the right thumb, a method of shooting still employed by Eastern archers to this day. A bone archer's ring can be seen in the Clayton Museum at Chesters and the method of using it is shown on page 39.

Arrow heads were being made in considerable numbers in a room of the head-quarters building at Housesteads in the fourth century. This does not imply that a corps or archers was in garrison for in the later Imperial army many units were trained in the use of the bow, slings, etc., it was after all an essential weapon for the defence of a fort and arrows were cheaper than javelins to produce and expend in large quantities (page 39).

The heads of heavy arrows or bolts shot from *ballistae* are common finds on Roman military sites in Britain. To see one of these bolts complete we must again turn to the remarkable finds from the mid third century defences of Dura Europos. There, in

Reconstruction of the chamfron from Newstead with eye-guards restored.

(*Below*)

Bronze auxiliary infantry helmet, late 1st-early 2nd century from the Rhine at Mainz.

Mittelrheinisches Landesmuseum, Mainz

Bronze shield boss of Germanic conical type from the Valkenburg fort, Holland.

Instituut voor Prae en Protohistorie, Amsterdam

Tower 19 of the defensive city wall, *ballistae* bolts were found with their wooden shafts and in one instance with its wooden flights complete (page 40). The fort at High Rochester which stands above the Jedburgh road (A68) north of Hadrian's Wall is an excellent example of a late fort with bastions for mounting pieces of artillery such as *ballistae* and the heavier and more powerful *onager* used for throwing stones. Some large stone shot survive adorning the little village school house at the foot of the hill leading up to the fort.

The Numeri and Cunei

The *numeri* and *cunei* were irregular troops who used their native weapons and were generally commanded by their own officers. As far as we can judge they were not in any way armed in the Roman manner though replacement arms may have eventually been made by Roman smiths and their appearance changed in consequence.

Units stationed on the northern frontier were of German origin such as the *numerus Hnaudifridi* based at Housesteads in the third century, from Holland the *cuneus Frisionum Aballavensium,* probably at Burgh-by-Sands (*Aballava*), and in·the third century at Papcastle. There were also vexillations or detachments from regular auxiliary units such as the *vexillatio gaesatorum Raetorum* of Swiss Celtic origin stationed at Greatchesters. These generally small bodies of men were used to reinforce existing garrisons or were based at forts and spent the greater part of their service patrolling the country beyond the frontier. A good example of this is the *numerus exploratorum Bremeniensium* attached to High Rochester fort in the third century.

One may picture these troops wearing their native tunics, trousers and boots, generally bareheaded or wearing simple caps and carrying shields, spears or javelins and perhaps a knife or sword. The detachment described as *gaesatorum Raetorum* were armed with the large Celtic javelin called a *gaesum,* a broad, barbed weapon with a slender neck and long socker such as was found at Carvoran and may now be seen in the Museum of Antiquities, Newcastle (page 40).

The equipment illustrated in this booklet and the reconstructions of the various types of troops described, may not conform with the popular conception of the Roman soldier but we must bear in mind that many changes took place in the third and fourth centuries. The unwillingness of Italians, and for that matter, citizens in provinces all over the Empire, to serve in the army, meant that recruits had to be sought elsewhere. The peoples of eastern Europe, particularly the Teutonic tribes from beyond the Rhine, filled the ranks of the legions, the auxilia and the new field armies. In the past the majority had only used a shield for defence and when they became Roman soldiers they brought with them an inborn reluctance to wear heavy armour.

Whilst cavalry units became more heavily armoured so as to withstand better the onslaught of the hordes of nomadic horsemen pouring in from the east, the infantry became steadily lighter armed in the manner of barbarian tribesmen against whom the Romans had fought and conquered in earlier centuries. Without armour, infantry could not stand up to attacks from armoured cavalry and so when late Roman commanders depended on such troops they frequently lost their battles and their armies.

Frontier troops such as those stationed on Hadrian's Wall maintained their traditions and often their armour through the fact that most of their recruits were local men or sons of serving or retired soldiers living in the vicinity of the forts.

Relief of a signifer or standard bearer of the early 3rd century from the fort at Carrawburgh. Clayton Museum, Chesters fort.

Photograph, Colin Butcher

The coloured plates show the equipment of these soldiers reconstructed

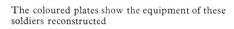

Gravestone of a Hamian archer from Housesteads, second quarter of the 2nd century.

Museum of Antiquities, Newcastle upon Tyne

Photograph, University Library and Museum of Antiquities, Newcastle upon Tyne

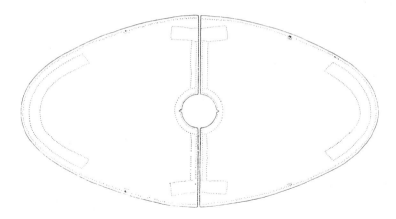

Diagram of a goat-skin cover for an oval shield from the fort at Valkenburg, Holland.

Instituut voor Prae en Protohistorie, Amsterdam

 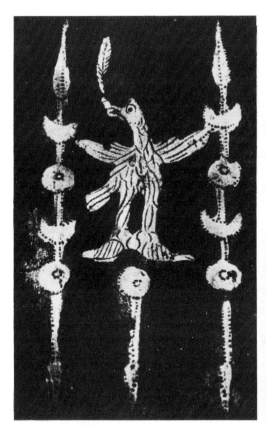

Bronze inlays in the fragment of a sword blade from South Shields.

(Left)   Obverse, the God Mars
(Right)   Reverse, legionary eagle and standards
Site museum.

Photograph, University Library and Museum of Antiquities, Newcastle upon Tyne

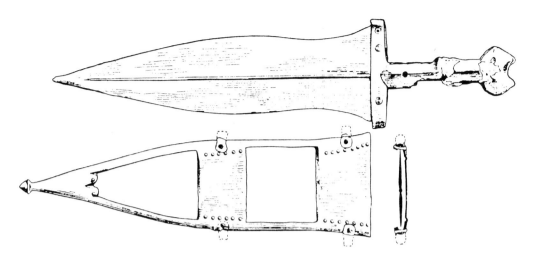

Large iron mounted dagger and sheath frame from Copthall Court, London, 3rd century.

Museum of London

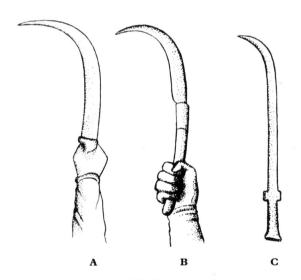

A   B   C

The Dacian sword.

A. & B.   As depicted on Trajan's Column, Rome

C.   As portrayed on the dedication stone from Birdoswald fort.

35

Bronze helmet for a cavalryman of *cohors equitata*, late 1st or early 2nd centuries.
Archaeological Museum, Zagreb

Photograph, R.G.Z.M., Mainz

Bronze helmet of a cavalryman of *cohors equitata*, late 2nd-early 3rd centuries, from Hönnepel. near Kleve.   German private collection.

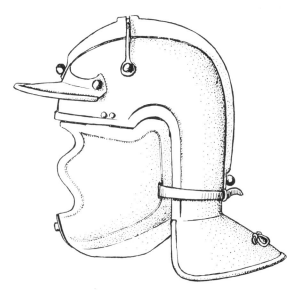

Conical bronze helmet of Syrian type, late 2nd century.   Archaeological Museum, Zagreb

Reconstruction with cheek-pieces restored from a pair found at Konigshofen near Strasbourg.

(*Opposite*) Cavalry officer and infantrymen of the 4th century

BRONZE HELMET FOR AN INFANTRYMAN *COHORS EQUITATA*, 2ND CENTURY

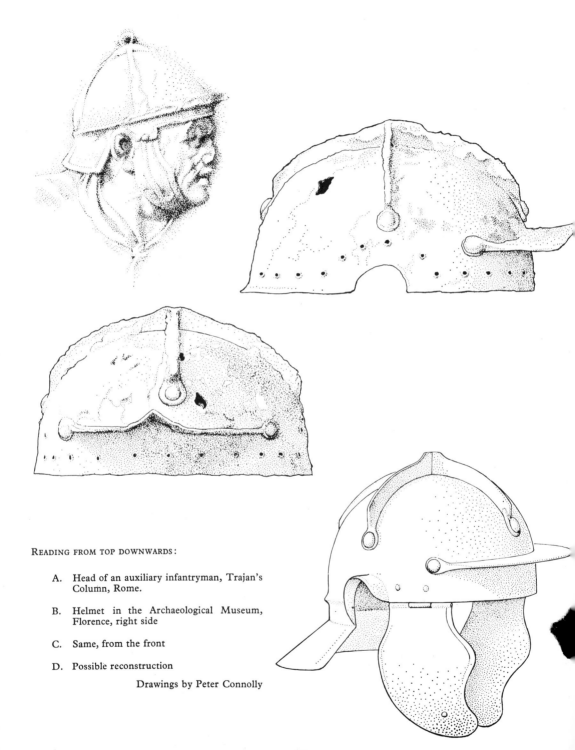

READING FROM TOP DOWNWARDS:

A. Head of an auxiliary infantryman, Trajan's Column, Rome.

B. Helmet in the Archaeological Museum, Florence, right side

C. Same, from the front

D. Possible reconstruction

Drawings by Peter Connolly